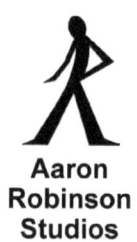

Aaron
Robinson
Studios

The Artwork of Aaron Robinson

Robinson and Malone Publishing, LLC
Contact: (312) 715-7884

Published 2019 by Robinson and Malone Publishing, LLC

ISBN: 9781798973264

Copyright © 2019 by Aaron Robinson
Cover Design by Aaron Robinson
Art by Aaron Robinson
Art Direction by Aaron Robinson
Edited by Tocarra Eldridge-Robinson

The information presented in this book solely and fully represents the views of the author as of the date of publication. Any omission or potential misrepresentation of any peoples or companies is entirely unintentional. As a result of changing information, conditions or contexts, this author reserves the right to alter content at their sole discretion impunity.

The report is for informational purposes only and while every attempt has been made to verify the information contained herein, the author assumes no responsibility for errors, inaccuracies, and omissions. Each person has unique needs and this book cannot take these individual differences into account.

All rights reserved. It is illegal to copy, distribute or create derivative works from this book in whole or in part. No part of this book may be reproduced or transmitted in any form whatsoever, electronic or mechanical, including photocopying, recording, or by any informational storage or retrieval system without expressed written, dated and signed permission from the author.

Table of Contents

Chapter 1
The Hip-Hop Theme, Pg 7

Chapter 2
Personal Experience In Art, Pg 14

Chapter 3
Females In Art, Pg 20

Chapter 4
Comic-Book Illustrations, Pg 24

Names and Descriptions of Artwork, Pg 31

Acknowledgement

First of all, I would like to thank God for giving me multiple talents. And one of those talents is being a fine artist. I would like to thank my wife Tocarra Eldridge-Robinson, and also my family and friends for their continued support. I would like to give a special thanks to Greg Samuel El, Mr. Collins, Mr. Wilson, Darryl Coleman and my mentor, the late Shenfield Dee. I would like to thank my former Lorenzo R. Smith art teacher Mr. Moore, and my former St. Anne Community High School art teacher the late Mr. Leon Savage. I also give thanks to my Kankakee Community College art instructors, Jane Haley and Jean Janssen, as well as my former Columbia College Chicago instructor Craig Jobson, along with a host of other educators and mentors. I also give a huge thanks to everyone who inspired me and gave me the opportunity to create and express myself, and every art exhibition, gallery, etc., that supported my work.

This book is dedicated to the late Mr. Leon Savage.

Introduction

The Artwork of Aaron Robinson is a book showcasing interesting art pieces. The content and work derives from an excursion of time that I, Aaron Robinson, author and fine artist, exceedingly articulates and expresses in my amazing artwork in several themes. I combine a trivial era that occurred in my life with art to highlight various personal experiences that I have encountered. While making a positive transition on my life's journey, I explore and discover to learn newly life lessons and personality, embodying my endeavors, trials-and-tribulations and challenges with my knowledge to discuss and paint a detailed, vivid and comprehensive description of multiple art pieces with my favorite art media that conveys a strong message.

Chapter 1 - The Hip-Hop Theme

Hip-hop is one of the many elements I utilize in my artwork. It gives me the freedom to express current events taking place in my life. Since birth, I have had a burning desire to pursue a career in music and performing arts, which now allows me to express my talent and creativity. As a result, my soul feels refreshed and alive.

As a child, when it was a challenge for me to express a vision or the way I felt, I would either draw a vivid picture or write lyrics. Somehow, I always found myself listening to the radio, inspiring me to work a music theme into my art.

The *Comprehend Character* is a graphite illustration of me as a hip-hop artist, representing my association with music. In the computer graphic illustration a boomerang which represents the knowledge of the hip-hop generation is placed in his hand. The boomerang is at 180 degrees meaning: the more knowledge you give the more you will receive once the boomerang is thrown and returns to you. *Self-Portrait*, a hip-hop personality, is a graphite drawing of me as an MC that was created by looking into a mirror.

The *Throw Ya Handzup CD Cover* is a computer graphic printout having the same effect which was later converted into *Throw Ya Handzup (t-shirt design)*. The hip-hop effect is still present, though a paint utensil was placed into his hands to combine the music and art theme.

B-Boy I is an original piece that was done in wire. In this sculpture, break-dancing is incorporated with a guy standing on his head. The urban feel is present and is very realistic. The cardboard and radio has a great amount of detail depicting the hip-hop culture also. *B-Boy II* is also detailed as well. A recorder is present along with a bible which is positioned in a box.

Cappadonna (Driving On) is an illustration of a rapper

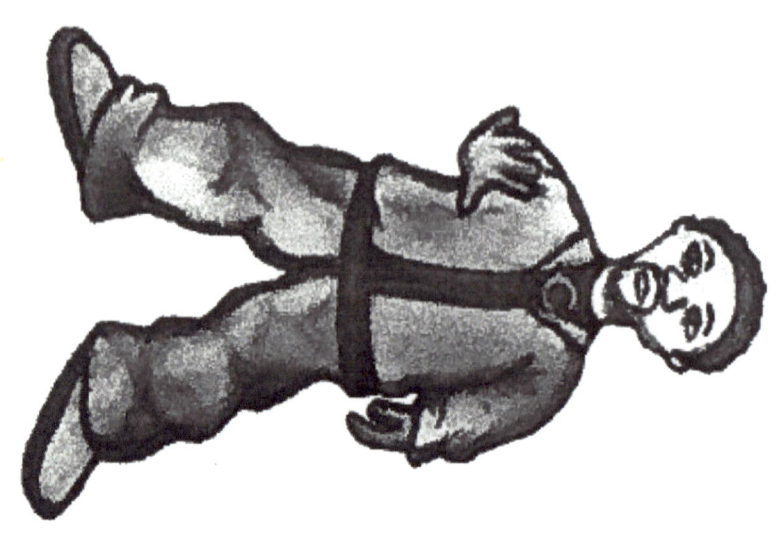

Comprehend Character

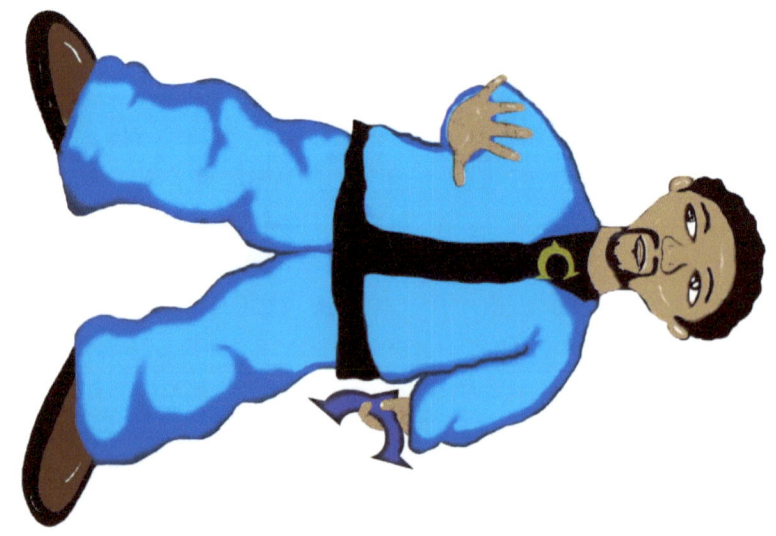

Comprehend Character

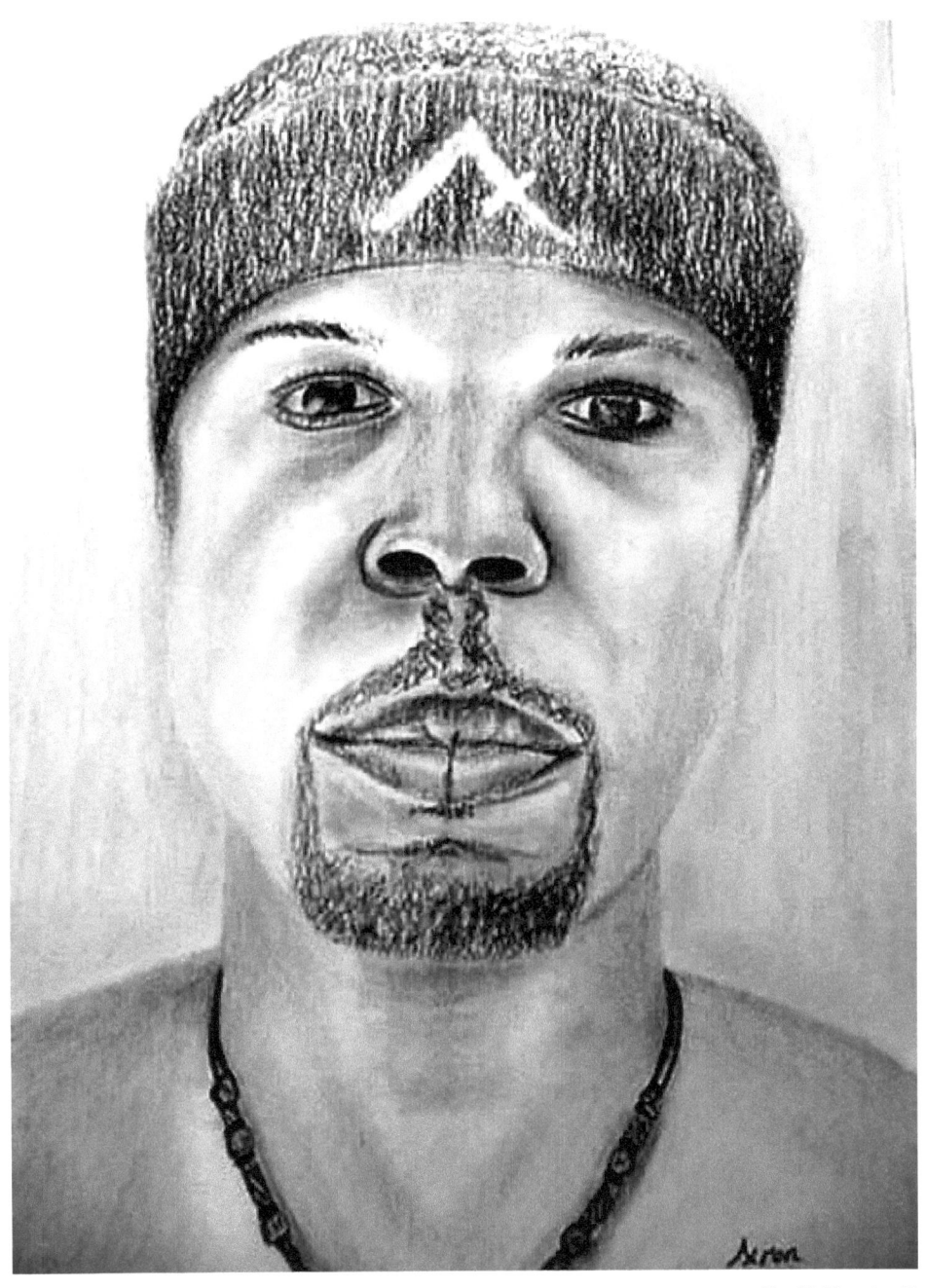

Self-Portrait

from Wu-Tang Clan. The illustration is from an original CD photographed cover. I enjoyed working on this piece because it is drawn in charcoal, and shade and shadow contrasting is one of my favorite techniques. Taking on this

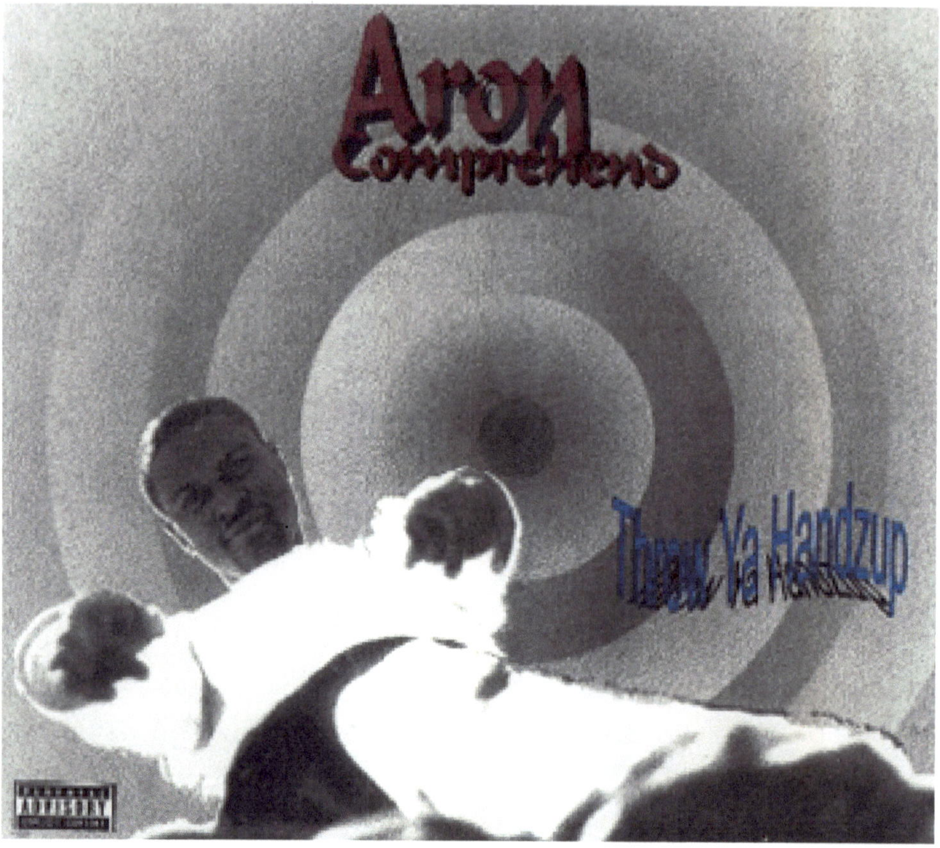

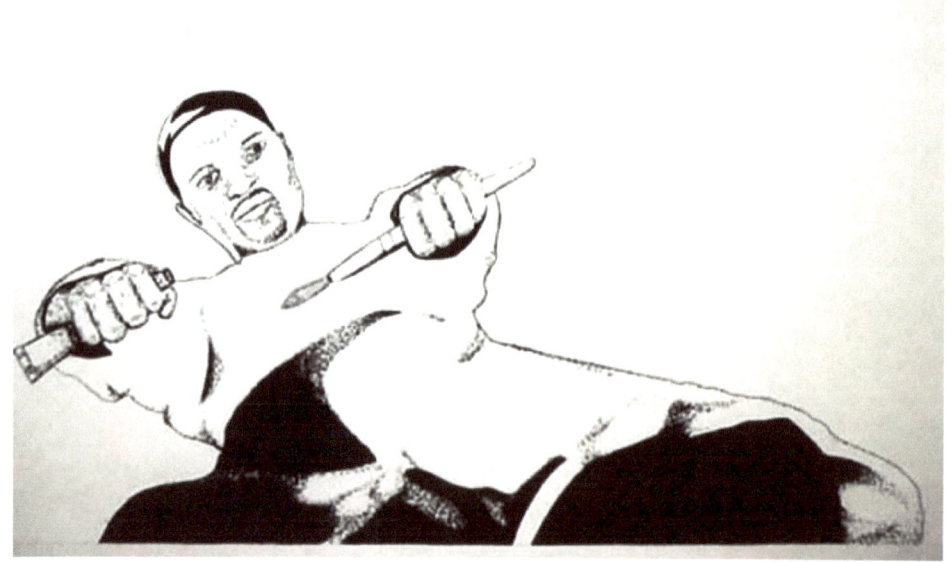

Throw Ya Handzup CD Cover

Throw Ya Handzup (t-shirt design)

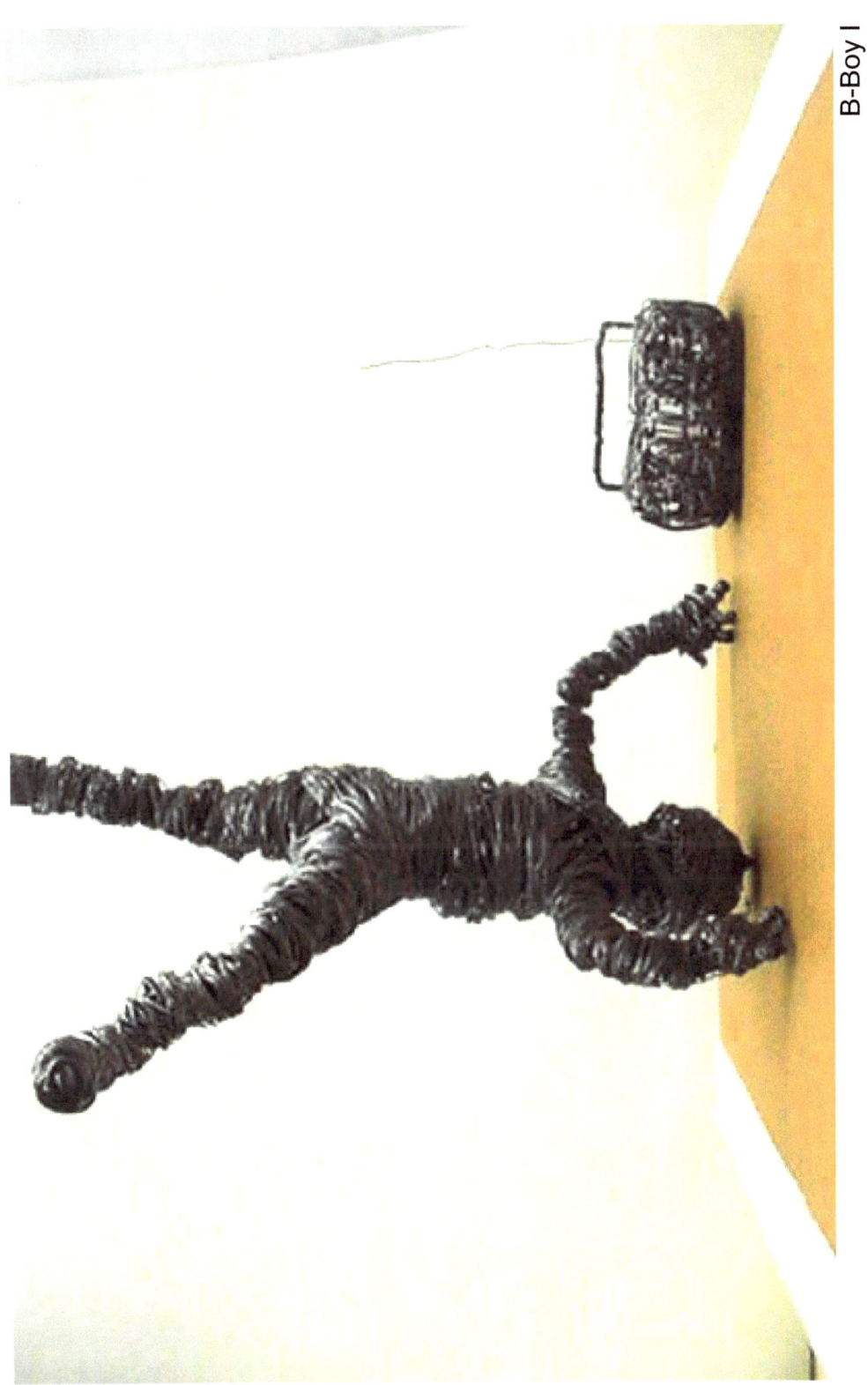

B-Boy I

project was a challenge and a great opportunity. However, my toughest challenge was overcoming the tragedy when my family's house burnt down and I lost this illustration. Though, I was grateful to have a copy of this piece published in a college newspaper before the unfortunate tragedy. I would say *Cappadonna (Driving On)* marks the first and new beginning for my art career in the theme of music and art.

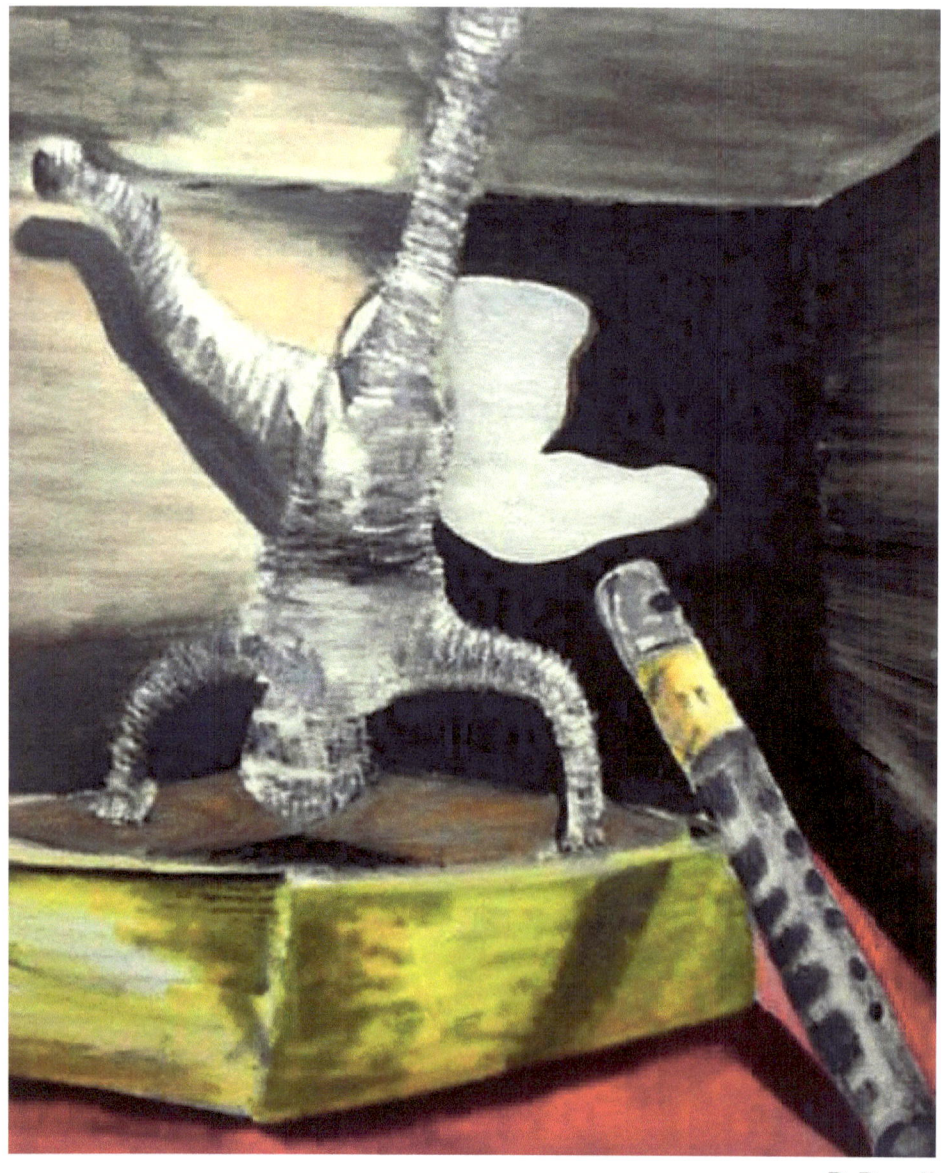

B-Boy II

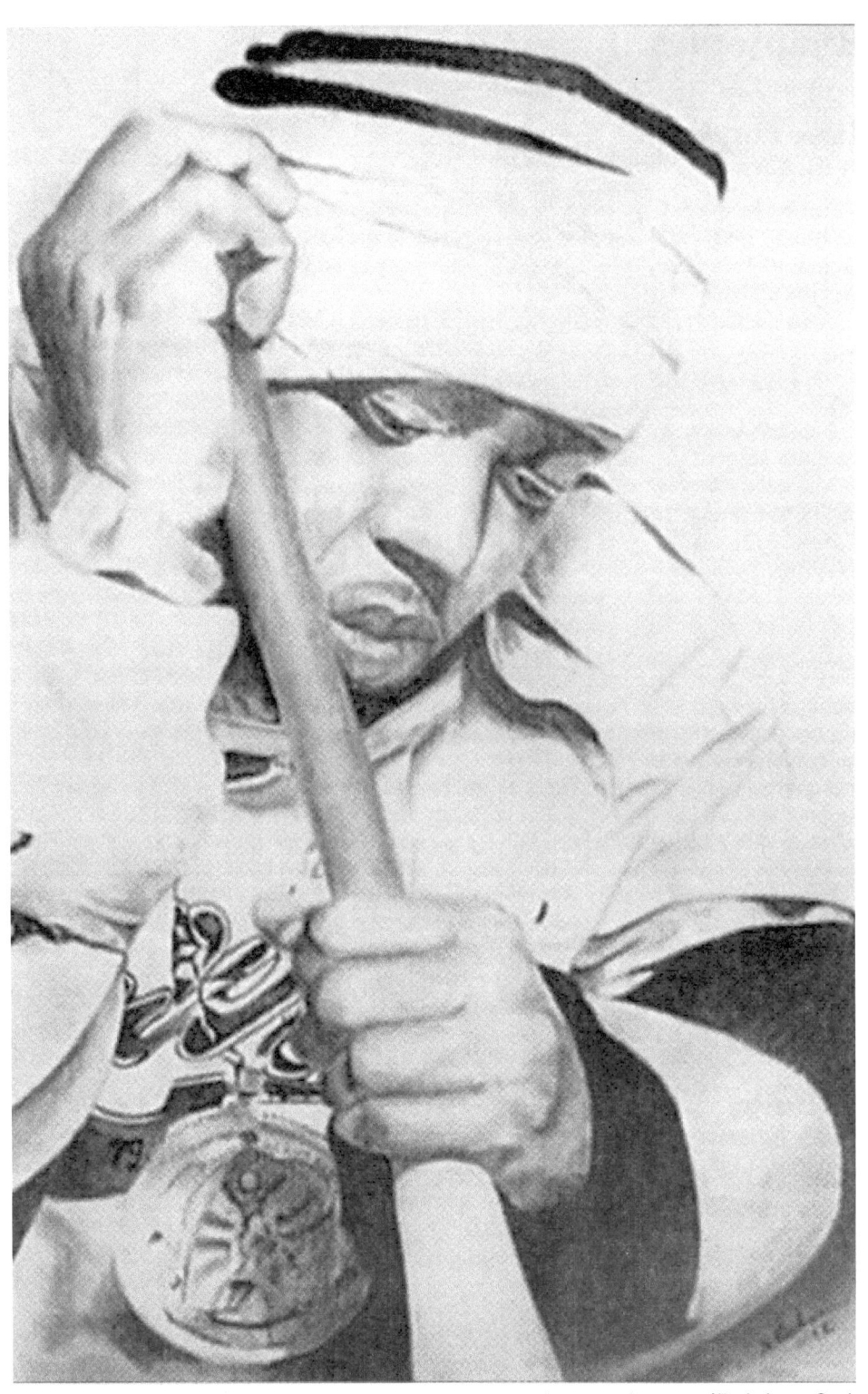

Cappadonna (Driving On)

Chapter 2 - Personal Experience In Art

In the majority of my work, I like to represent spiritual themes which may be perceived as religion concepts. As an artist, I'm really conscious of my surroundings and enjoy touching people's lives with my artwork that derives from my beliefs and personal experiences.

Peaceful Journey is one of my groundbreaking illustrations. It depicts a time of my life when I discovered the light and was searching for wisdom and understanding. In order to incorporate this in other illustrations, I had to study my heritage and roots to discover who I was as an individual. Converting all negativity that existed in my thought process into positivity played a major role. I also discovered the majority of my understanding through meditating, reading, and being humble. Once I grasped understanding, the world was becoming more clear to me.

The Vision depicts clarity or the right-of-passage - the transition of going from one mental state of mind to another. The grassland indicates where I once was in my life time; the water symbolizes the new decisions and choices I began to make in my life as I navigated toward the mountains which represent light or destiny. When I discovered the light, I understood that my world belongs to me just as it is represented in *Mattsini I (Matt: 6.9)*, *Mattsini II*, and *Mattsini III*.

Mattsini I gives a sense of giving the world to someone. It's having heaven on earth. *Mattsini II* was created from an awkward experience. It was as if I predicted moving to Chicago before I moved there. This oil painting is an excursion of time, life, and maturity. I say this because I was born and partially raised in Chicago for a certain amount of time and was removed from the city at a young age. When I matured and received a sense of direction in

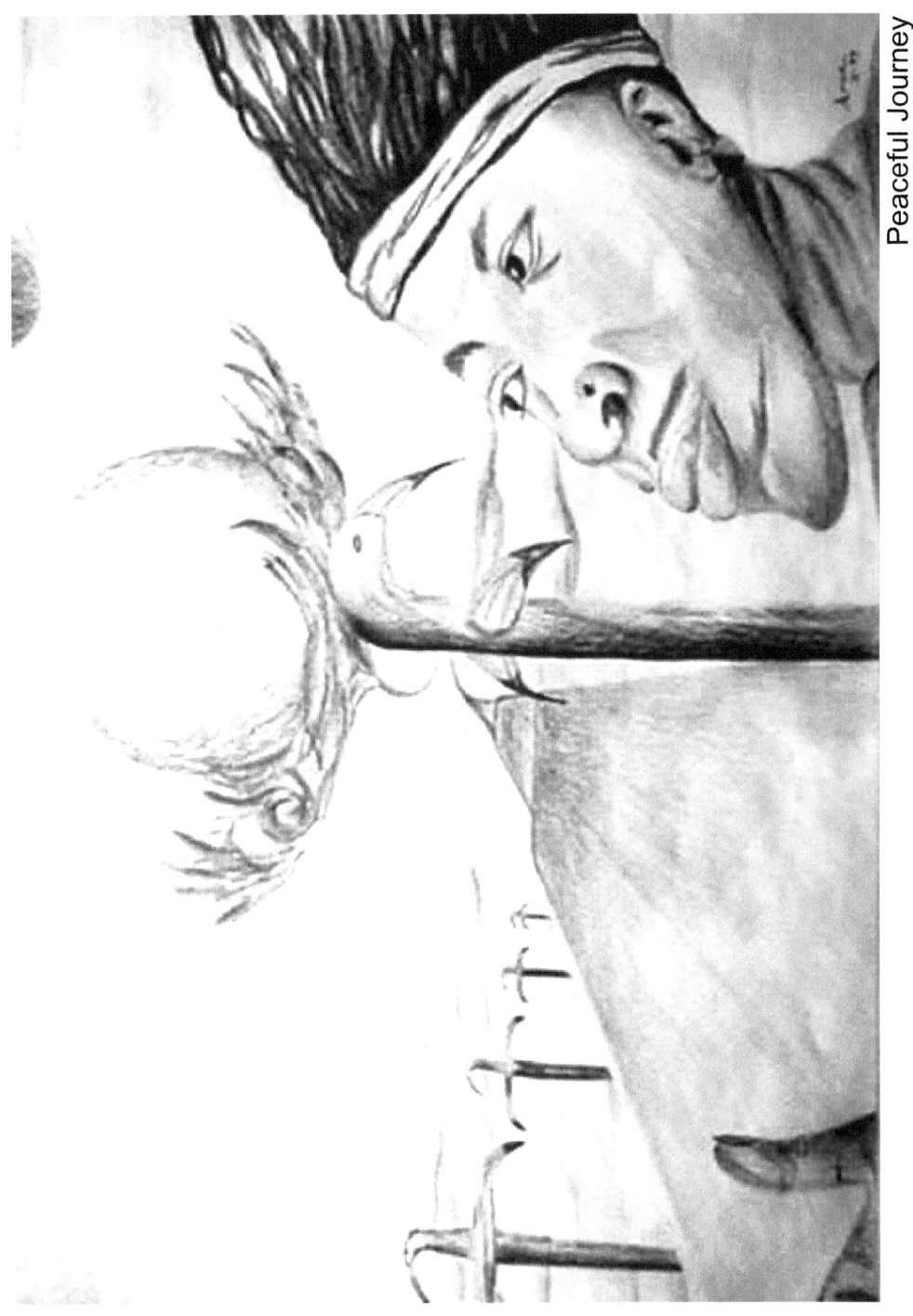

Peaceful Journey

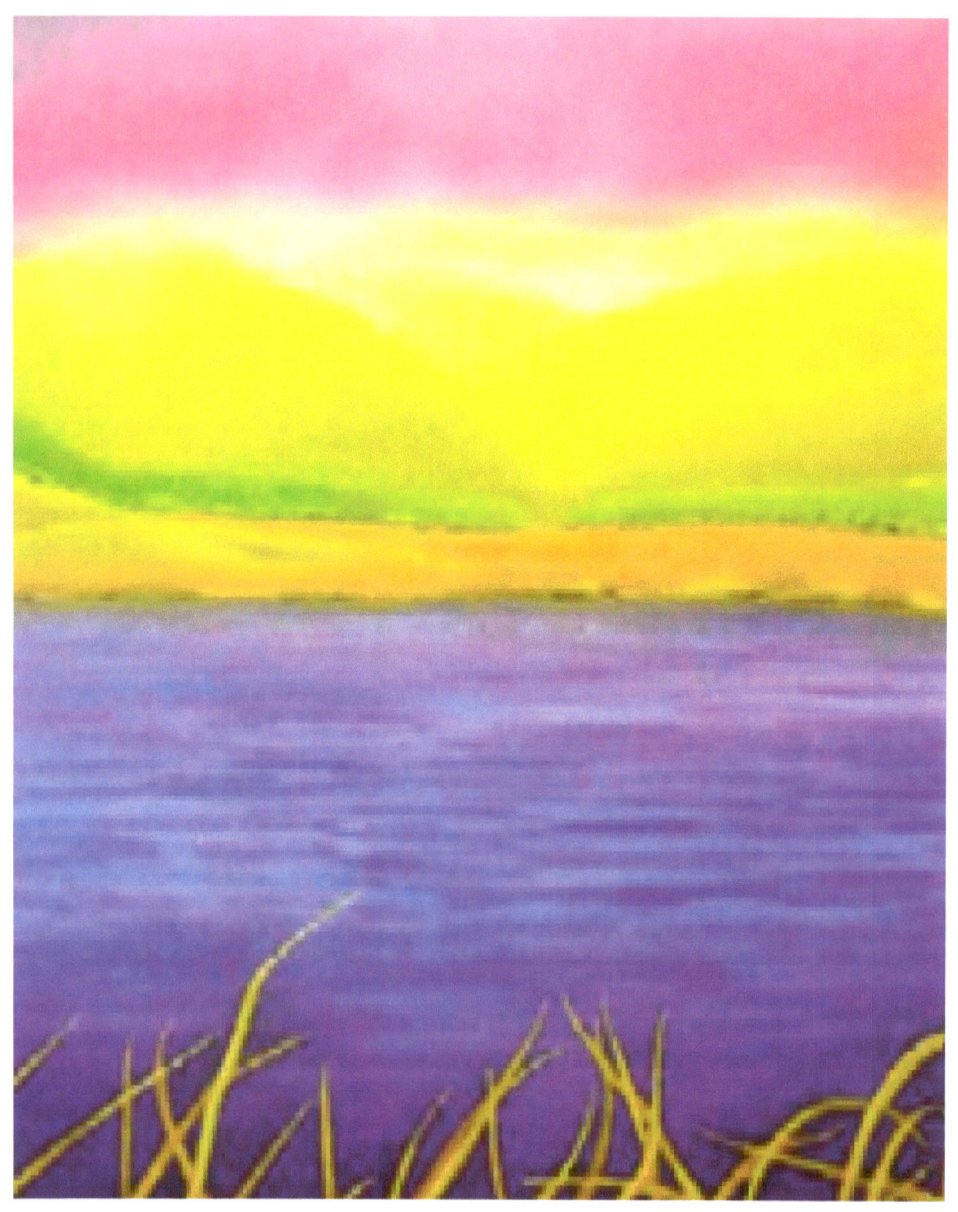

The Vision

life, I went back to conquer and explore. Since this painting is the 2nd of a triptych, I take you inside of my world and take you out of space in *Mattsini III*. The face and hands represent a spiritual guy praying for the world. His locks represent knowledge and culture, as well as the guy in *Mattsini II*. The earth which is half of a spear demonstrates the knowledge that most people may have on earth.

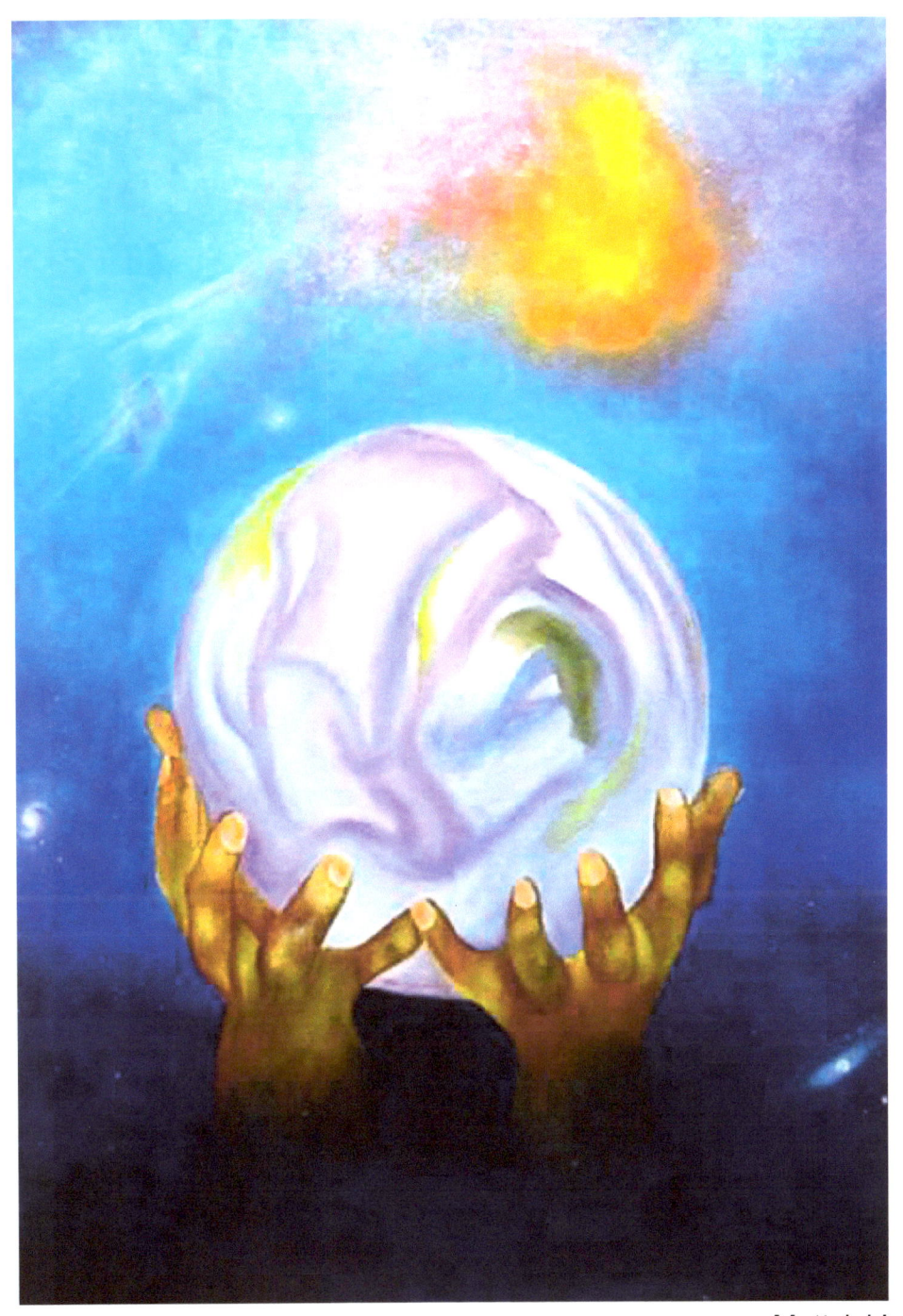

Mattsini I

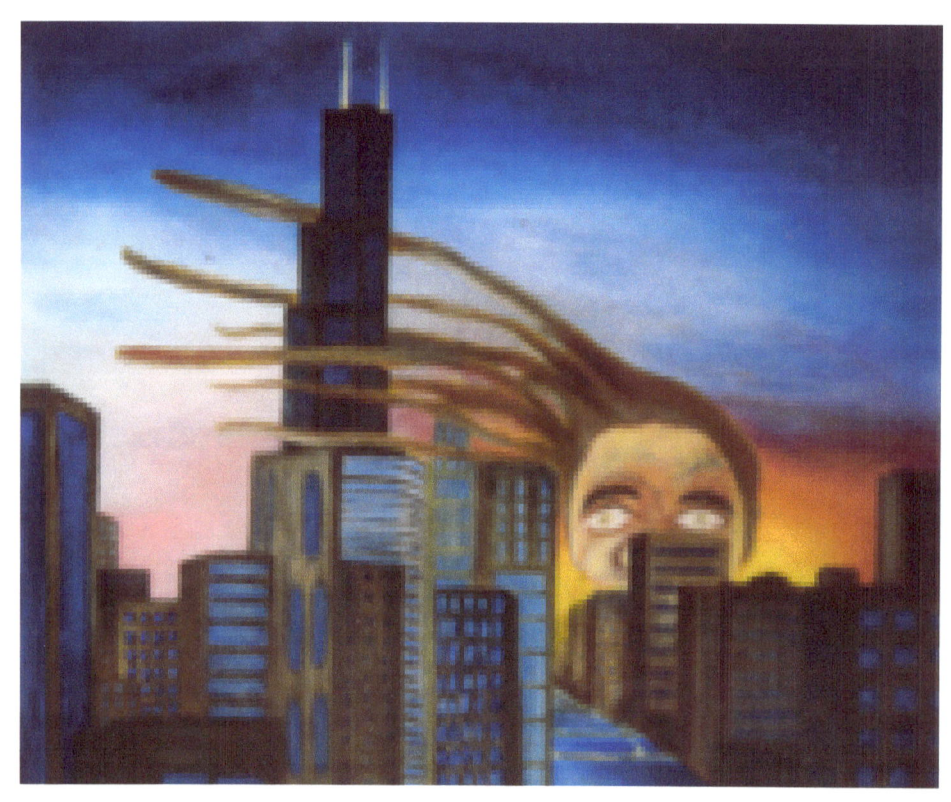

Mattsini II

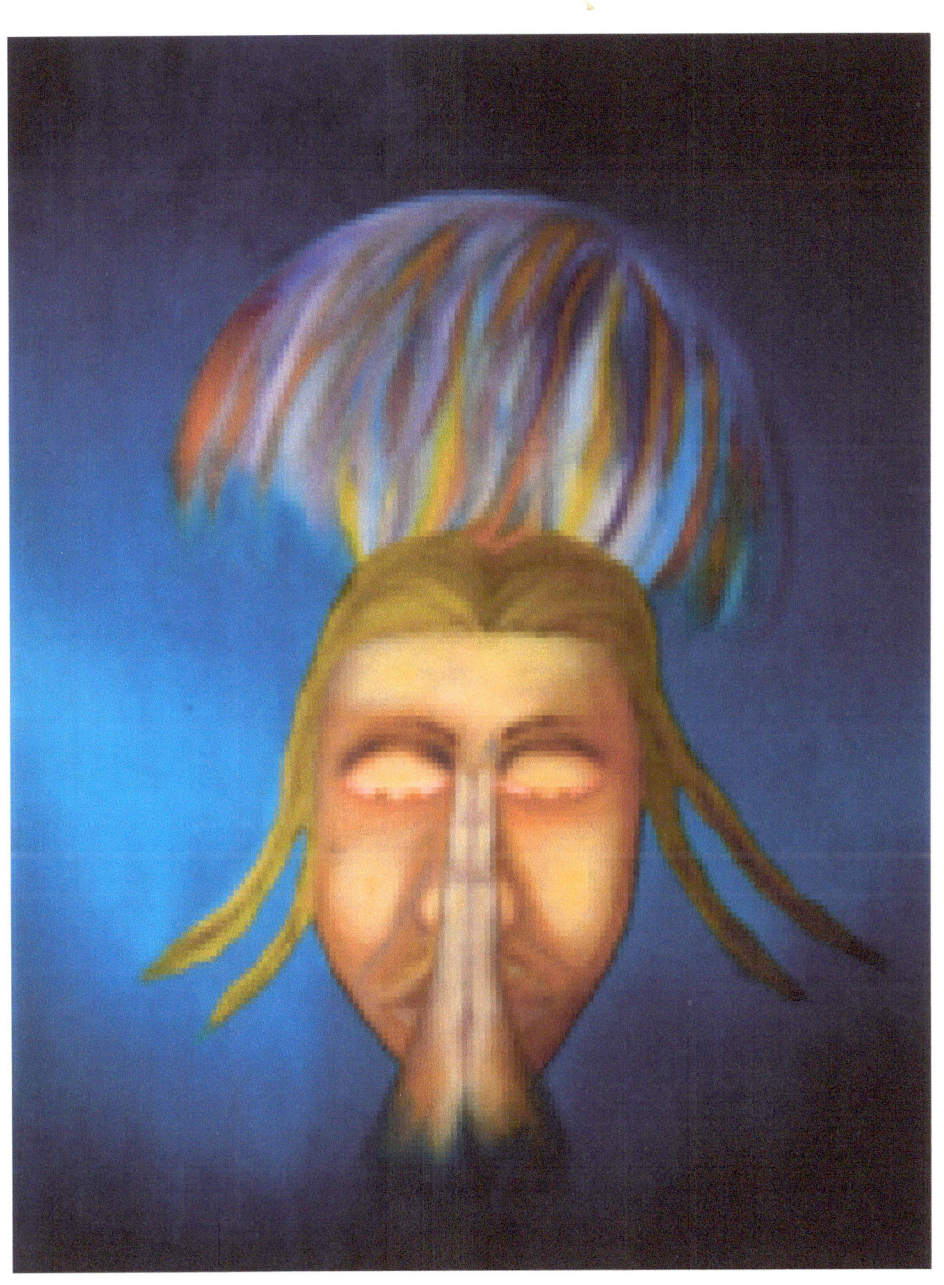

Mattsini III

Chapter 3 - Females In Art

In this chapter, I demonstrate my belief of women. Don't get me wrong, I love women, but a man can only endure so much. This may be true for women in many cases as well. I illustrated my ideas in detail while creating these paintings and drawings.

False Faces consist of a collage of women faces that have unique characteristics. Again, the painting is based on my belief of women which I demonstrate by symbolizing the colors of the faces, eyes and mouths. These elements compliment each other by giving the painting a good and evil look while representing how women are viewed in everyday life.

I enjoyed working on *Ground Zero* I. The theme is sort of futuristic, using boxed characteristics that look like robots to represent interpretation. Sometimes it is hard for a person to let go of someone due to the fact that he/she may become attached to an individual. Usually an individual will let go or fall down, eventually he/she will rise. Elevating is what I represent in *Ground Zero II* in which I demonstrated two box women standing on the man while bowing down to his sphere. The spear is an interpretation of the man's knowledge who overcame from trials-and-tribulations from his past experiences with women. Now he is able to take control of his environment and has the experience to serenade and meet new women.

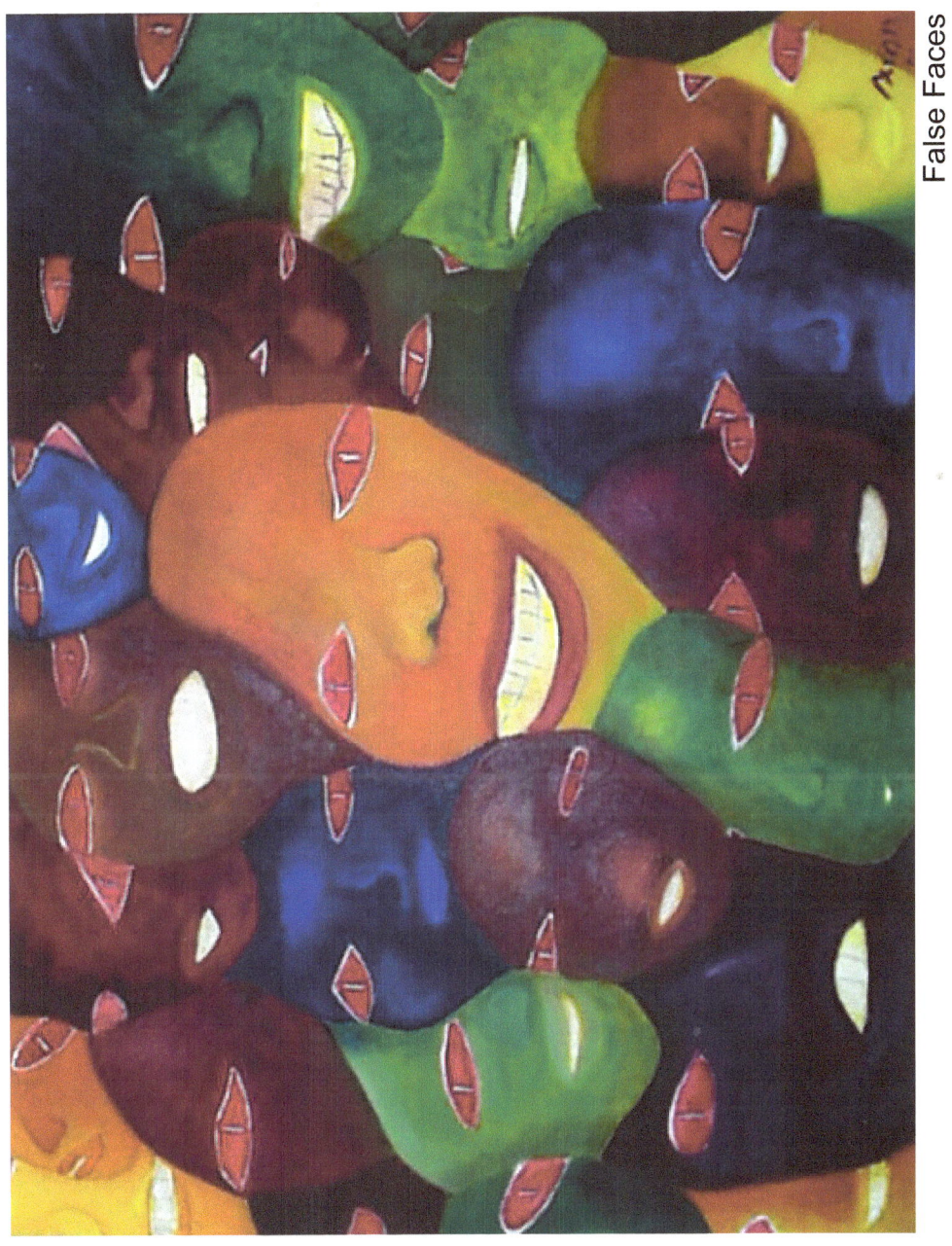

False Faces

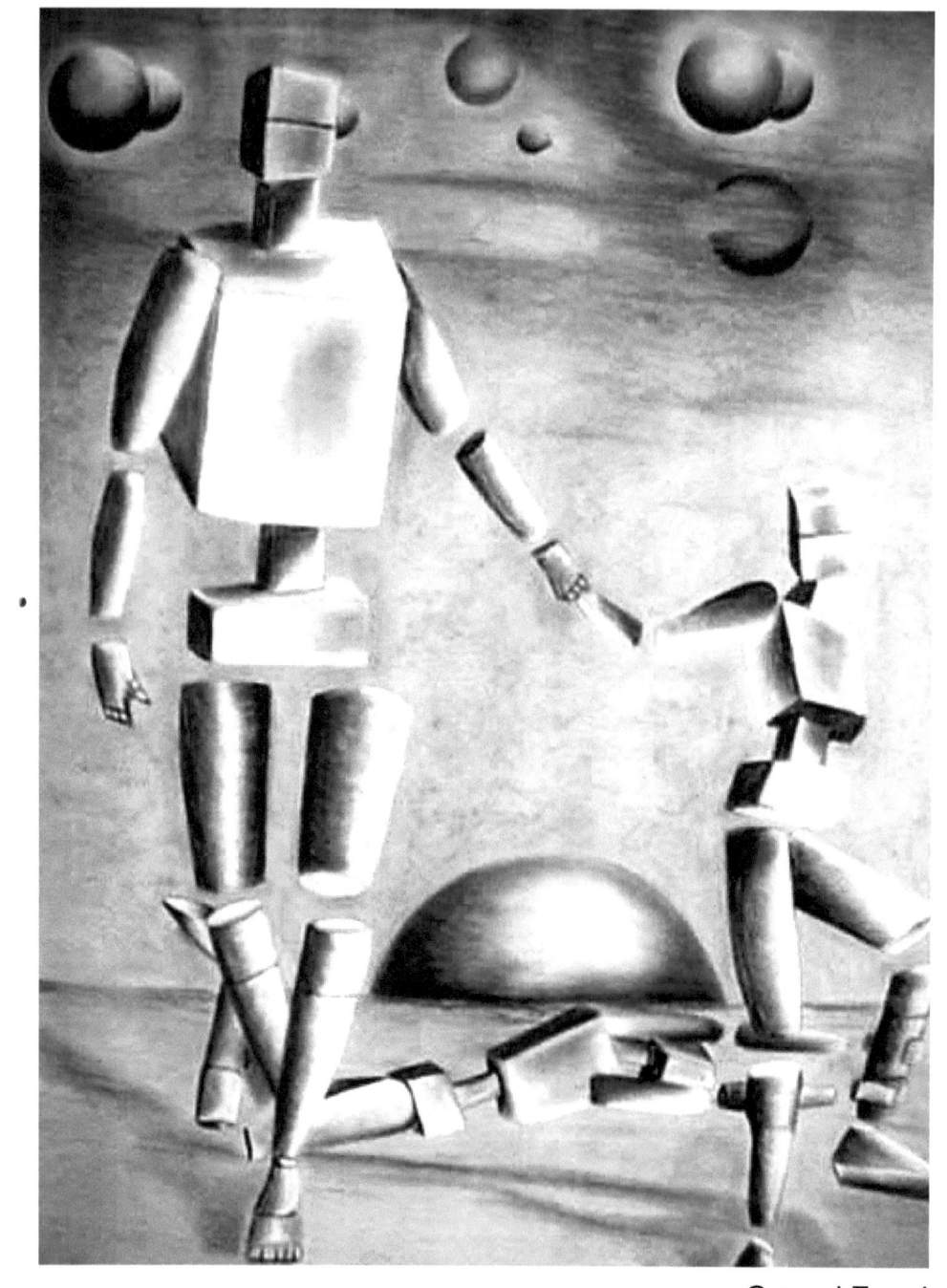

Ground Zero I

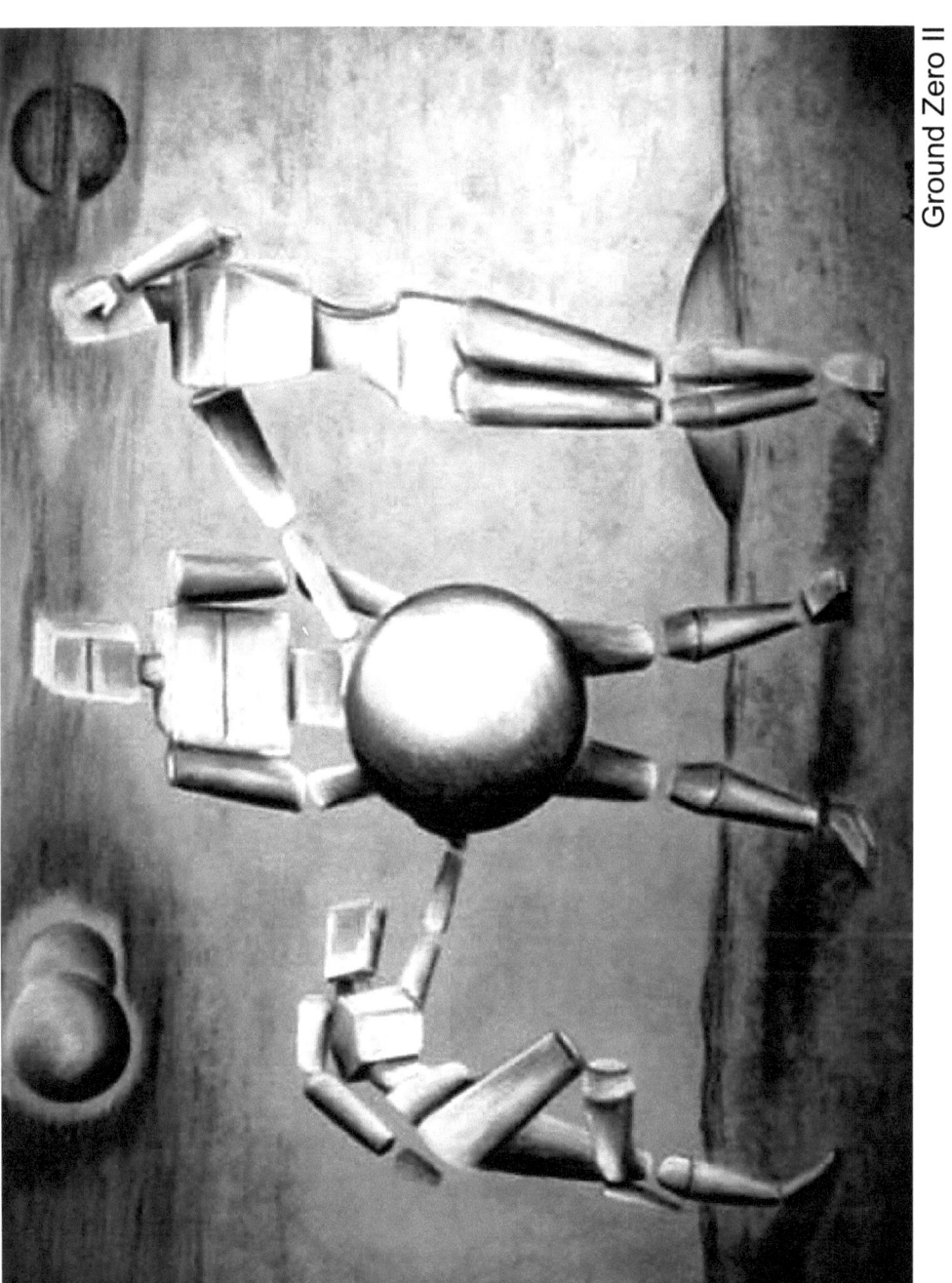

Ground Zero II

Chapter 4 - Comic-Book Illustrations

I enjoy spending my time working on comic book characters, supporting them with a dramatic story. In the past, many characters I mimicked by drawing for practice or to past time by, has always given me the opportunity to develop personality and style.

Gabriel is a character I did for hire. This militant character was extremely fun creating, yet very time consuming. The character is drawn with ink and stands in a "ready for war position."

Seaman is a character that was taken from my future comic-book Earth Global Domes, a comic-book based after the nuclear war around 2037. *Seaman* lives underwater in a dome and operates many administrations and makes executive decisions. The character may have room for improvement in the future and may have to go through a few computer graphic transitions. The illustration is created in colored pencils while *Seaman's Body Positions* are created in graphite.

Dejackey Ru is also a character taken from the comic-book Earth Global Domes. It is sketched in colored pencils. The character is a twin of another character who is dressed in camouflage colors. The character has a tattoo illustrated on his body suggesting the group he resides in after the nuclear war. The *Dejackey Ru* is also illustrated in *Dejackey Ru's Body Positions* capturing various positions of his body form.

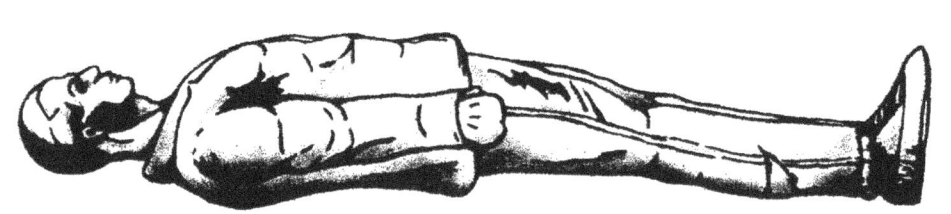

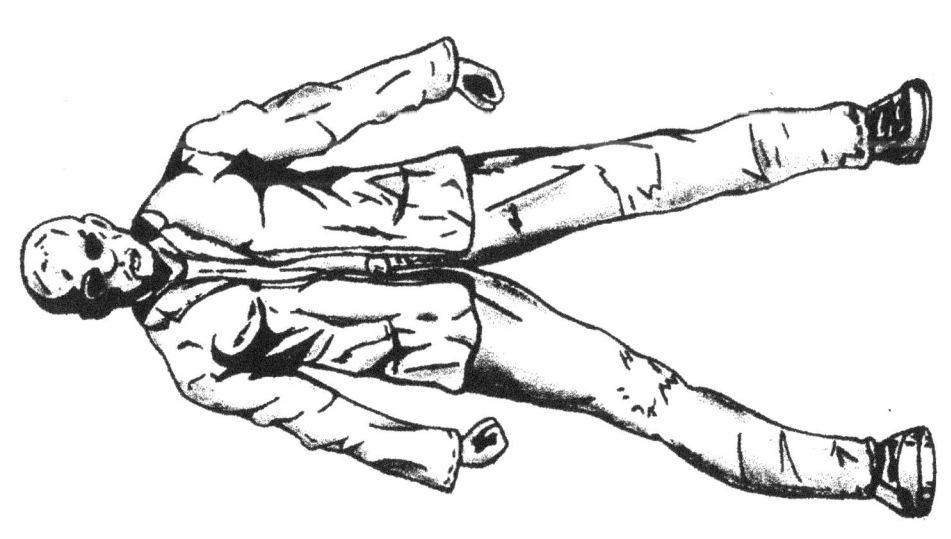

Gabriel

The Artwork of Aaron Robinson

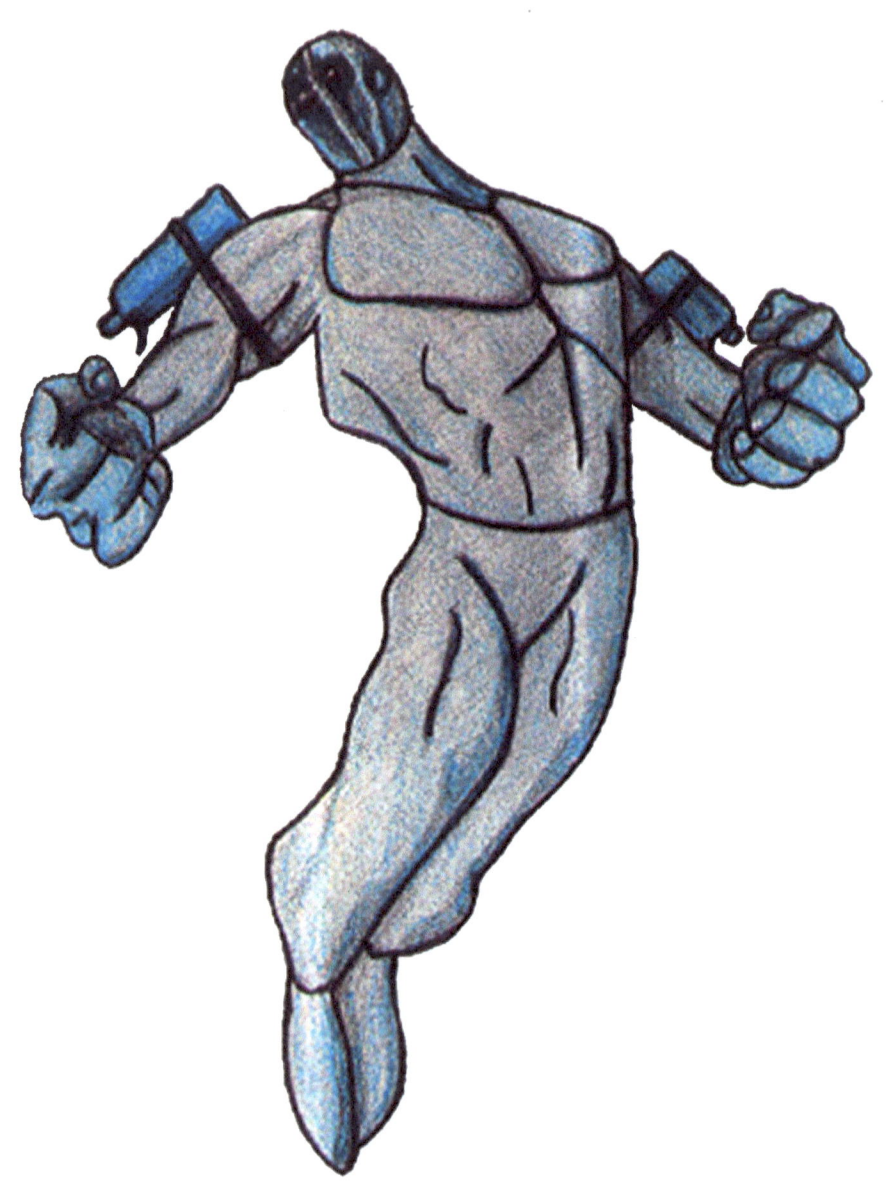

Seaman

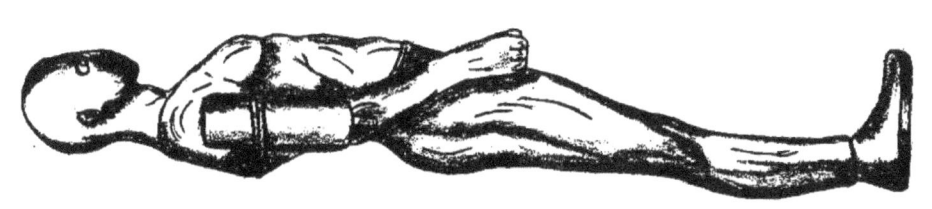
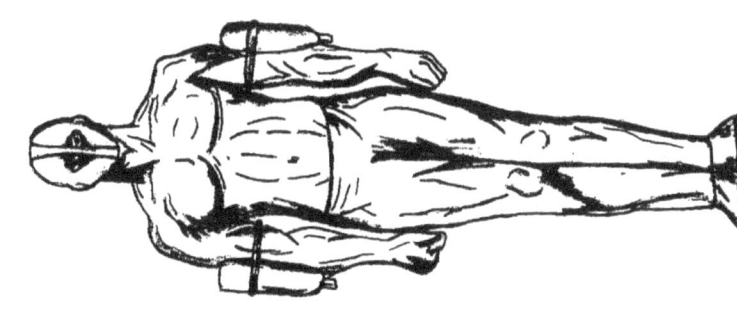
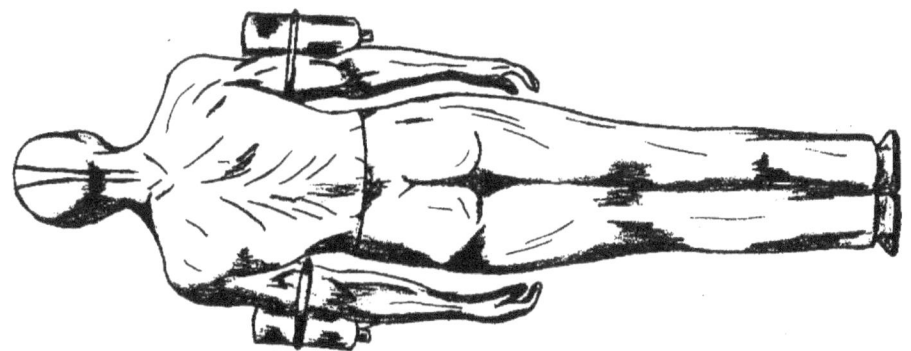

Seaman's Body Positions

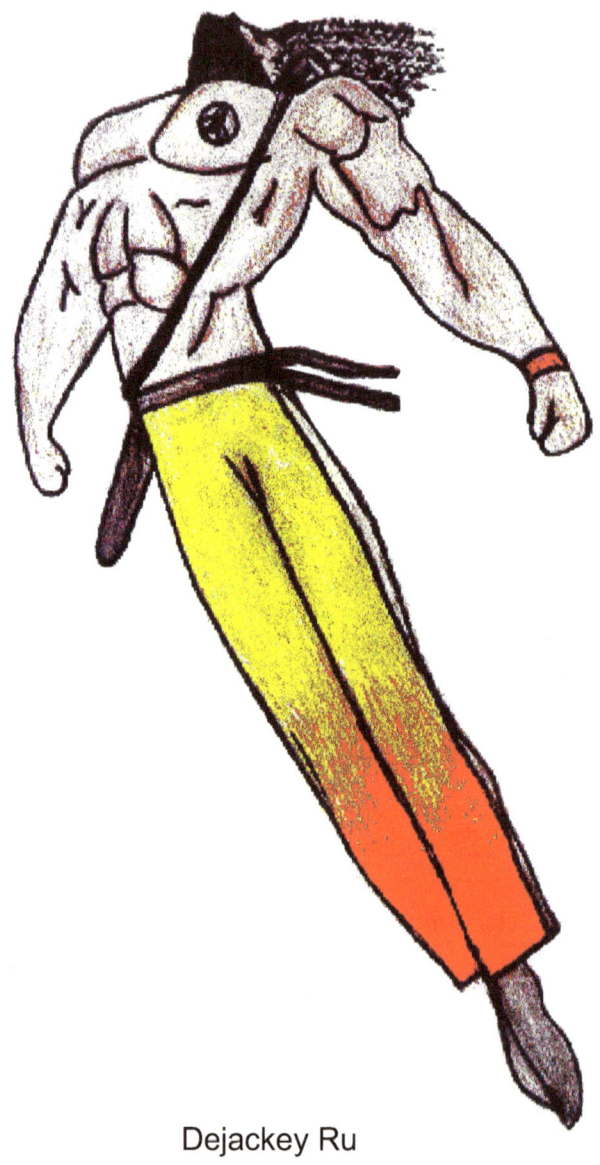

Dejackey Ru

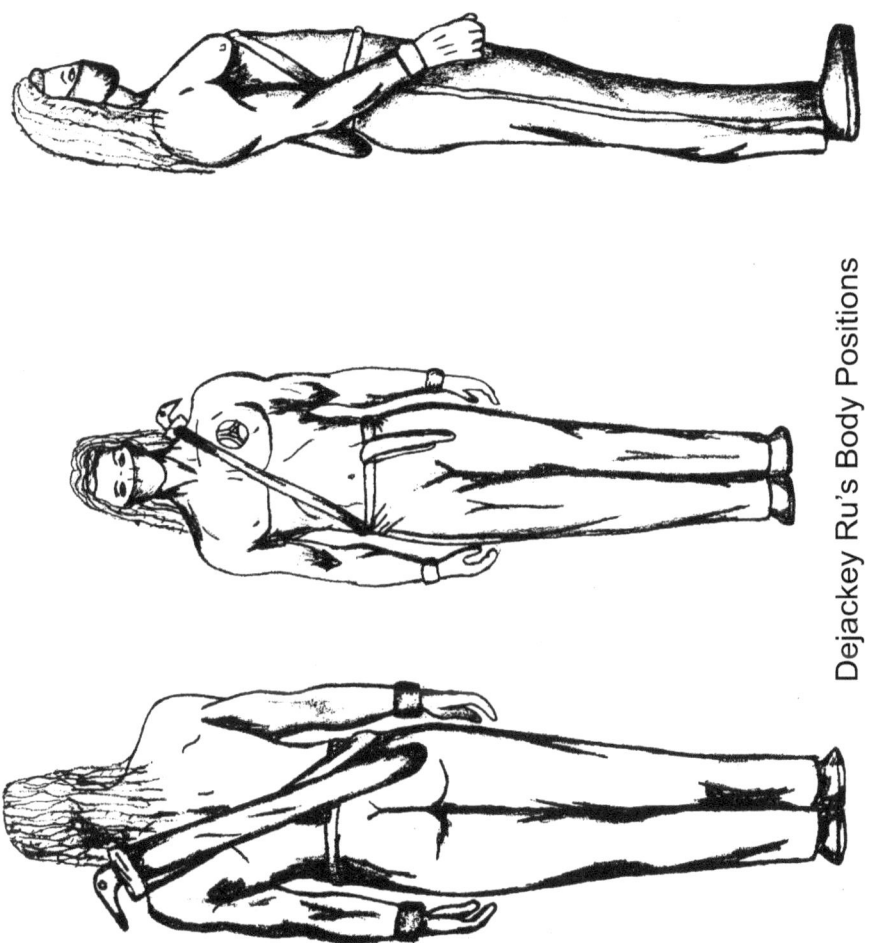

Dejackey Ru's Body Positions

Summary

Overall, I like to express myself by using a variety of elements in my artwork. These elements may derive from hip-hop, personal experiences, females, or comic book illustrations; though, the subject matter of these illustrations are usually related to one another depending on its theme. There are a wide variety of media I enjoy working with, but I prefer charcoal and oil paint due to the fact that it is fun to work with and easy to maneuver. I also enjoy working with computer graphic layouts such as comic book characters and CD cover layouts, which is an avenue I'm constantly exploring in my art career. As long as I can create, I will continue to make a positive impact on people's lives.

Names and Descriptions of Artwork

Comprehend Character, 1 ¾ x 4 ¾ graphite on white paper - pg. 8
Comprehend Character, (computer graphics) 1 ¾ x 4 ¾ - pg. 8
Self-Portrait, 15x 20 graphite on illustration board - pg. 9
Throw Ya Handzup CD Cover, (computer graphics) - pg. 10
Throw Ya Handzup (t-shirt design), 20 x 15 gouache on illustration board - pg. 10
B-Boy I, wire sculpture - pg. 11
B-Boy II, acrylic paint on canvas - pg. 12
Cappadonna (Driving On), 15 x 20 charcoal on illustration board - pg. 13
Peaceful Journey, 25 ½ x 19 ½ graphite on white paper - pg. 15
The Vision, 18 x 22 oil on canvas - pg. 16
Mattsini I, 24 x 30 oil painting on canvas - pg. 17
Mattsini II, 30 ½ x 24 ½ oil painting on canvas - pg. 18
Mattsini III, 22 x 28 oil painting on canvas - pg. 19
False Faces, 30 x 24 acrylic paint on canvas - pg. 21
Ground Zero I, 23 x 29 charcoal on gray paper - pg. 22
Ground Zero II, 23 x 29 charcoal on gray paper - pg. 23
Gabriel, 6 x 1 ¾ ink on illustration paper - pg. 25
Seaman, colored pencil on white paper - pg. 26
Seaman's Body Positions, graphite on white paper - pg. 27
Dejackey Ru, colored pencil on white paper - pg. 28
Dejackey Ru's Body Positions, graphite on white paper - pg. 29

Aaron Robinson Biography

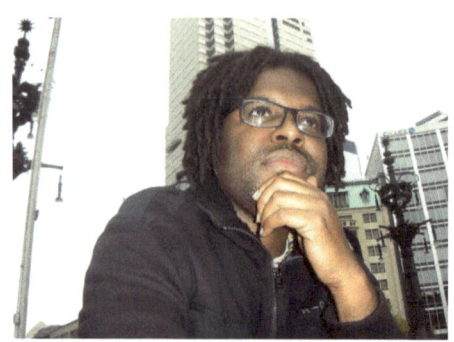

Aaron Robinson is the Chief Executive Officer of Robinson Publishing Incorporation, which produces the national magazine titled Consciousness Magazine, as he has the creative role as Editor/Publisher for over 14 years. He is the art director of Allezom International Magazine and ultimately assists with the development process of numerous publications around the world.

Robinson attended Columbia College Chicago, holding a Bachelor's degree in Fine Arts and Science and an Associate's degree in Fine Arts. He has nearly two decades of experience as a magazine publisher and over 15 years of experience as a professional graphic designer, where he designs local and national projects.

Robinson has been a guest speaker at universities, colleges and high schools lecturing on topics concerning publishing and graphic designing. He is also the founder and Operations Manager of the youth nonprofit organization Still I Rise and holds a seat on the Developing A Neighborhood Master Plan board in his local community. As a businessman, he continues to collaborate on various business ventures, striving to be diverse as an entrepreneur, making a substantial contribution to the art and publishing world as an innovator and philanthropist.

Robinson and Malone Publishing, LLC
Contact: (312) 715-7884